A GIFT FOR

_____

FROM

_____

If Only I Knew...

LANCE WUBBELS

GIFT BOOKS

To

Spencer Ingvalson

The precious boy

who loved his yellow bike . . .

and his mother dearly.

You touched so many lives

for one so young.

INTRODUCTION

While I was writing this book, the fourteen-year-old son of a friend of mine left home on his yellow bicycle, heading for soccer practice as he had countless times before, and was hit broadside in a street crosswalk by a car. The driver, a sixteen-year-old young man, was distracted and somehow never even saw Spencer until he hit the windshield. In that tragic moment, a boy's life vanished like a mist, leaving behind a grieving mother who obviously loved him with all her heart.

We live in an uncertain world. When we leave home in the morning, we assume we will return in the evening. When we say good-bye to loved ones, we take it for granted we will see them again. We presume they know we love them, so we seldom say the words. Unfortunately, we fail to consider the mortal reality that this may not be the case . . . until it's too late. Tomorrow does not always come.

Someone once said that "life is short, so keep short accounts with God." That is wise advice, but I'd like to add that we should also keep short accounts with every person who is in the circle of our lives. We never know when life will be dramatically changed . . . sometimes permanently.

Think about it. Don't allow the regrets of "if only I knew" to be the final marker of your life. Be swift to love. Hurry to be kind. Take the time to make someone feel special. Freely give hugs and kisses, and may "I love you" be often on your lips.

Lance Wubbels

"Be devoted to one another in brotherly love. Honor one another above yourselves.... Share with God's people who are in need. Practice hospitality. Bless those who persecute you; bless and do not curse. Rejoice with those who rejoice; mourn with those who mourn. Live in harmony with one another.... Do not be conceited. Do not repay anyone evil for evil. Be careful to do what is right in the eyes of everybody. If it is possible, as far as it depends on you, live at peace with everyone."

ROMANS 12:10-18

IF ONLY I KNEW...

I would never hear your voice again,

I would cherish your every word . . .

every inflection of your voice . . .

with all my heart.

IF ONLY I KNEW . . .

THIS WAS OUR LAST HUG,

I WOULD HOLD YOU TIGHT

AND HOPE TO NEVER LET YOU GO.

IF ONLY I KNEW...

this was the last time...

the very last time...

I would see you,

I would take the time

to treasure everything about you.

If Only
I KNEW

I had the chance to

pray with you

one more time,

I would take your hands

and welcome God's presence

to surround us.

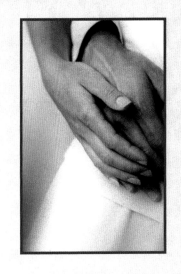

IF ONLY I KNEW

that disagreements do not mean

a lack of love,

I would have been hurt less often.

IF ONLY I KNEW . . .

THAT EVEN WHEN EVERYTHING IN MY LIFE

SEEMS TO GO WRONG

AND COMES CRUMBLING DOWN AROUND ME,

EVEN WHEN MY HEART IS BROKEN,

GOD HAS PROMISED

TO ALWAYS BE WITH ME.

If Only I Knew...

HOW **OFTEN** AND HOW BADLY

I HAD MISJUDGED PEOPLE,

I WOULD HAVE OPENED MY HEART MORE OFTEN

TO LOVE

AND BE LOVED.

IF ONLY I KNEW . . .

that no one ever

sees the same thing

in exactly the same light,

I would have found

more pleasure

in others' opinions,

even when they did not share mine.

If Only I Knew . . .

that I was powerless to change other people,

I would have stopped trying

and been free to love them

for who they were,

flaws and all.

IF ONLY I KNEW . . .

THAT MOMENTARY PLEASURES

COULD RUIN A REPUTATION FOR A LIFETIME,

I WOULD HAVE FOUND THE STRENGTH

TO SAY NO TO TEMPTATION.

If Only I KNEW . . .

TOMORROW WAS NOT COMING,

I WOULD ASK YOU

TO PLEASE FORGIVE ME

FOR ANY WRONG I MAY HAVE DONE TO YOU.

If Only I Knew . . . THIS WAS OUR FINAL KISS,

I WOULD USE IT

TO TELL YOU THAT YOU ARE

THE LOVE OF MY LIFE.

IF ONLY I KNEW . . .

I could never share

another day with you,

I would make the most of every second.

IF ONLY I KNEW . . .

THIS WAS THE LAST GIFT

I COULD GIVE YOU,

I would surprise

you with something

THAT SAYS NOTHING

COMPARES WITH YOU.

If Only I Knew...

THAT MIRACLES DO HAPPEN,

I WOULD CLING TO GOD

WITH ALL MY HEART AND SOUL.

IF ONLY I KNEW . . .

that I was caught in the trap

of living for tomorrow

and a future that existed

only in my imagination,

I would have slowed my pace,

drawn boundaries around my work,

and taken time for the people I love.

IF ONLY I KNEW...

my choices...

however small and seemingly insignificant...

were taking me away from you,

I would turn around and run to you.

If Only I KNEW . . .

your hand would

never hold mine again,

I would wish this moment

would never end.

IF ONLY I KNEW . . .

MY VOICE

WAS ABOUT TO GO SILENT,

MY WORDS TO YOU

WOULD BE PUNCTUATED WITH

"I LOVE YOU'S."

IF ONLY I KNEW . . .

that a break in our relationship

might go unresolved,

I would do everything

within my power to mend it.

If Only I Knew...

THAT NO WORD OF LOVE IS EVER LOST,

I WOULD HAVE ALLOWED MY TONGUE

MORE FREEDOM TO TRULY SPEAK

FROM MY HEART.

IF ONLY I KNEW . . .

the destructive power

of gossip,

slander,

and talking behind

other people's backs,

I would have chosen

my words

more carefully.

IF ONLY I KNEW . . .

THAT SOMETIMES IT'S BETTER NOT TO KNOW,

I WOULD HAVE SPARED MYSELF HEARTACHES

AND CARES I WAS NEVER MEANT TO CARRY.

If Only
I KNEW

that my past is no excuse

for who I am now,

that truth could have

set me free to change.

IF ONLY I KNEW . . .

THAT SUCCESS IS NEVER MEASURED

IN DOLLARS OR POSITIONS,

I WOULD HAVE TREASURED

THE THINGS THAT LAST FOREVER.

IF ONLY I KNEW . . .

that wonders surround all we do . . .

everywhere . . .

all the time,

I would have searched

my little corner of the world

and been continuously amazed.

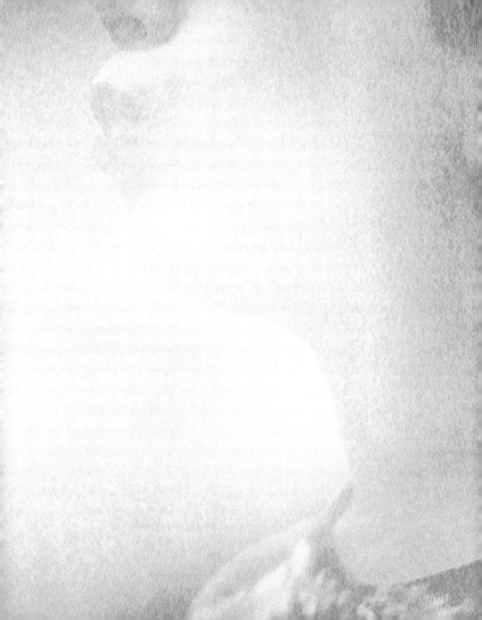

IF ONLY I KNEW . . .

THAT GRIEF AND HEARTACHE

COULD BE SO DEEP

AND DEVASTATING,

I WOULD HAVE BEEN THERE

MORE OFTEN FOR OTHERS.

If Only I Knew...

THAT BASKETS OF BELIEFS

ARE OF LITTLE VALUE,

I WOULD HAVE MADE CERTAIN

THAT MY BELIEFS

WERE TURNED INTO CONVICTIONS

THAT SET THE COURSE OF MY LIFE.

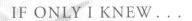

IF ONLY I KNEW . . .

that others were watching my life as an example,

that my life was influencing others,

I would have asked God to shape my character

to be a reflection of His heart.

IF ONLY I KNEW...

THAT EVEN

A CHILD'S DAYS

ARE SOMETIMES CUT SHORT,

I would wish

for more long nights

OF ROCKING YOU

TO SLEEP.

If Only I Knew...

THAT IT WAS WRONG

TO PUT OTHERS

UNDER MY OWN EXPECTATIONS

AND MAKE THEM FEEL GUILTY,

I WOULD HAVE STOPPED

MANIPULATING THEM

AND CHOSEN LOVE

AS THE HIGHER WAY.

IF ONLY I KNEW . . .

HOW LITTLE

I ACTUALLY UNDERSTOOD ABOUT YOU,

I WOULD LISTEN CLOSER

TO YOUR WORDS,

SEARCH OUT YOUR THOUGHTS,

AND SEEK TO KNOW

THE DEEPEST DESIRES

OF YOUR HEART.

If Only

I KNEW

that my memories

of you would be

so precious,

I would take the time

to carefully gather your life story.

IF ONLY I KNEW . . .

that anyone can bring

words of comfort,

encouragement, and healing,

who knows how many lives

I might have touched?

If Only I KNEW . . .

THAT FRIENDSHIPS ARE SO PRECIOUS,

I WOULD HAVE NEVER TAKEN

ANYONE FOR GRANTED . . .

ESPECIALLY YOU.

IF ONLY I KNEW...

our phone call was the last we'd ever have,

I would speak only

loving words.

IF ONLY I KNEW...

I was about to lose your smile,

I would thank you

for all the joy you've brought to my life.

If Only I KNEW . . .

THE LOVE AND STRENGTH AND SUPPORT

YOU'VE ALWAYS GIVEN ME

WERE ABOUT TO END,

I would run to your

side and thank you

FOR THE MILLION TIMES

YOU'VE MADE A DIFFERENCE . . .

THE DIFFERENCE . . .

IN MY LIFE.

If Only I Knew...

THAT GOD CREATED ME FOR A PURPOSE,

I WOULD HAVE

PASSIONATELY SOUGHT HIM

TO DISCOVER WHAT

HE DESIRED.

IF ONLY I KNEW

that it's never too late to rewrite one's life story,

I would have pulled out my pen sooner.

IF ONLY I KNEW . . .

that when God closes a door,

He opens another,

I would have been less afraid of change

and more welcoming

of new opportunities and adventures.

If Only I Knew...

THAT STICKING WITH IT

IS A WAY OF LIFE,

I WOULD HAVE LEARNED MORE

FROM MY FAILURES AND SETBACKS.

If Only

I KNEW

GOD GIVES US A LIFETIME

TO BECOME THE PERSON

HE WANTS US TO BE,

I WOULD HAVE BEEN MORE PATIENT

WITH MYSELF . . .

AND OTHERS.

—

IF ONLY I KNEW . . .

THAT SOMETHING

SO STUPID AND WRONG

would hurt you

so badly, I WOULD TAKE A STAND

AND NEVER LET IT HAPPEN.

IF ONLY I KNEW...

that it is not enough

to empty my life of wrong,

but to fill it with things that truly matter.

If Only
I KNEW

that everything depends upon

what you believe,

and that ignorance

is no excuse,

I would have been more vigilant

to put truth into my heart.

If Only I Knew

HOW OFTEN I BLINDLY ACCEPTED

ANOTHER'S BELIEFS,

COPIED SOMEONE ELSE'S LIFE,

AND TRIED TO IMITATE

THEIR SPIRITUAL EXPERIENCE,

I COULD HAVE FOUND MY OWN

AND MADE THEM REAL.

IF ONLY I KNEW

that the love of God . . .

knowing God loves me . . .

reaches into my fears and insecurities,

I would have allowed His love

to surround,

engulf, and pierce

into the depths of my soul.

IF ONLY I KNEW. . .

that real happiness is a state of mind,

and that there's no substitute

for a good attitude,

I would have been more thankful for what I had,

and the chance to live and to work and to love.

If Only
I KNEW

THERE IS SO MUCH MORE TO LIFE

THAN BEING SAFE,

I WOULD HAVE BEEN QUICK

TO GIVE MYSELF TO OTHERS.

If Only I Knew

THE DEPTHS OF WISDOM

AND INSIGHT POSSESSED BY PEOPLE

AROUND ME,

I WOULD HAVE SPOKEN LESS AND LISTENED MORE.

If Only I Knew

THIS WAS OUR LAST WALK,

I WOULD TRY TO EXPRESS

MY FEELINGS FOR YOU,

EVEN THOUGH MY WORDS

HAVE ALWAYS BEEN INADEQUATE.

If Only I Knew...

I COULD NEVER TUCK YOU INTO BED AGAIN,

I WOULD CUDDLE YOU TIGHT,

REFUSE TO RUSH,

AND ENJOY THE WONDER

OF BEING WITH YOU.

If Only I Knew

MY DAYS WERE COMING TO AN END,

I WOULD NUMBER THEM CAREFULLY . . .

ONE BY ONE . . .

AND ASK GOD TO HELP ME

MAKE THE BEST USE OF MY TIME

BECAUSE THE DAYS ARE FAR TOO FLEETING.

LANCE WUBBELS is the vice president of literary development at Koechel Peterson & Associates, a Minneapolis-based design and publishing firm. Before joining Koechel Peterson, he served for eighteen years as managing editor at Bethany House Publishers.

Wubbels has authored several fiction and non-fiction books, including the Angel Award-winning novel *One Small Miracle* and the Gold Medallion-winning devotional *In His Presence*. *If Only I Knew* is his first book for Hallmark.

He and his family make their home in Minnesota.